Hearing

Written by Mandy Suhr
and
Illustrated by Mike Gordon

WAYLAND

The Senses

Hearing
Sight
Smell
Taste
Touch

First published in Great Britain in 1993
by Wayland (Publishers) Ltd

This edition printed in 2001 by Hodder Wayland,
an imprint of Hodder Children's Books
Revised in 2007 by Wayland, an imprint of Hachette Children's Books

Series Editor: Mandy Suhr
Consultants: Jane Battell and Richard Killick
Cover Designer: Elaine Wilkinson

British Library Cataloguing in Publication Data
Suhr , Mandy
 Hearing - (Senses series)
 I. Title II. Gordon, Mike III. Series
 612.8

Paperback ISBN 978-0-7502-5275-1

Printed and bound in China
Hachette Children's Books, 338 Euston Road, London NW1 3BH

Contents

Listen to the sounds around you.
What can you hear?

Some sounds are quiet and peaceful.

Some sounds are loud
and noisy.

Some sounds make
you feel happy.

Some sounds make
you feel cross.

Sounds travel through the air but you can't see them.

You use your ears to hear them.

The outer part of your ear catches the sounds and sends them down a hole. This hole leads to a tunnel that goes right inside your ear.

At the end of the tunnel there is a thin bit of skin. This is stretched tight across the end of the tunnel, just like the skin on the top of a drum.

This is called your ear-drum.

When the sounds hit your ear-drum they make it wobble or vibrate, just like when you hit a real drum.

When your ear-drum vibrates, it makes
3 tiny bones inside your ear move too.

These little bones send messages
through a long curly tube, called
the cochlea, to your brain.

The messages go to your brain along special paths called nerves. Then your brain works out what the sounds are.

Some animals can hear better than people. My rabbit Lucy is very good at hearing with her long ears. She can even move them about to help her find out where sounds are coming from.

Dogs can move their ears too. They prick up their ears so that they can 'catch' the sounds more easily.

20

Dogs are very good at hearing. They can even hear some sounds that people can't hear.

When you have a cold you can't hear so well because your ears are all blocked up.

But your hearing soon
comes back as you
get better.

23

My friend Rachel is deaf. This means that she can't hear very much at all. She wears a special hearing aid that helps her and she watches my lips to see what I am saying.

But she's still the fastest runner
in the school!

Very loud sounds can harm our ears so we have to look after them carefully.

26

Some people work in very noisy places. They have to wear ear-muffs to stop their ears from being hurt.

What sounds do
these things make?

Can you copy these sounds?
How many other sounds can
you make?

Notes for adults

'The Senses' is a series of first information books especially designed for the early stages of reading. Each book has a simple, factual text and amusing illustrations, combining reading for pleasure with fact-finding.

The content of the book addresses the requirements of the National Curriculum for Science, Key Stage One. The series takes a closer look at the human body, explaining very simply how we use each of our senses to learn about the world around us. This book explores the sense of hearing.

The books are equally suitable for use at home or at school. Below are some suggestions for extension activities to complement the learning in this book.

1. Design a hearing game using the one in this book as an example. This activity promotes collaborative learning when carried out in small groups. It encourages dicussion and hypothesising, both important language skills. Children can also be encouraged to design a scoring system to incorporate practise of numerical skills.

2. Practise grouping and ordering skills. Sounds can be grouped and then ordered within their group according to loudness. This involves designing experiments, discussion, using mathematical sets and provides a variety of opportunities for recording of results eg. graphs, tables, setting up and using data bases.

3. Collate and compose poems and descriptive writing using onomatopoeia, ie., that use words which sound like the thing they are describing. These could also be put to musical scores made by the children.

4. Use a drum to demonstrate the workings of the ear drum. Children will actually be able to feel the vibrations caused when the skin of the drum is hit.

5. Find out about other creatures that can hear well. Compare the way they hear to that of humans.

Books to read

Hearing by Henry Pluckrose (Franklin Watts, 2001)

Making Sounds by M. Perham and J.Rowe (Franklin Watts, 2004)

My First look at Noises by Toni Rann

(Random House Children's Books, 1991)